WRITING FOR THE NEW GENERATION

MORISSA SCHWARTZ

Morissa Schwartz

GenZ Publishing

2015® Morissa Schwartz

All rights reserved. No part of this publication may be reproduced, distributed, or transmitted in any form or by any means without the prior written permission of the publisher, except in the case of brief quotations and other noncommercial uses permitted by copyright law. For permission requests, write to publisher at GenZPublishing@gmali.com

ISBN: 0692613854

ISBN-13: 978-0692613856

GenZPublishing.org

Aberdeen, NJ

~To all those who deserve to have their voices heard~

Morissa Schwartz

Contents

Guiding Lite 7
Pleased to Meet You 10
The Times are Always A-Changin' 16
Write, Alright? 20
Sustained Silent Reading Time 22
Get Creative 25
Be Not Afraid 32
Grammar Rules! 35
    So, But, and…And 38
Be Concise, B-E Concise 40
    Very 48
Vary Your Language 49
Write Mindfully 52
Using Rhetorical Devices 54
Editing and Proofreading 55
A Brief Break 57
Book Length 76
Judging a Book by Its Author 78
Social Media and You 84
Write Expert 87

Morissa Schwartz

Guiding Lite

This is your guide to writing. Full of English *cheat codes* and *life hack*s to make your job as a writer simpler and to ensure that you will succeed at your mission of spreading your thoughts, words, and ideas with the world.

In this guide, you will see many links that will take you to particular websites and web tools. These are my personal favorites, and they are free, so take advantage of them. You will also see a lot of quotes from established writers. As Marlene Dietrich put it, "I love quotations because it is a joy to find thoughts one might have, beautifully expressed with much authority by someone recognized wiser than oneself." When we read our own thoughts in the form of those writers who we admire, it shapes us to be better writers by reestablishing or reshaping our thoughts. We grow, and when we grow our writing evolves.

Morissa Schwartz

Members of generation Z and millennials have many amazing tools that we can and should use. We have more technology than our ancestors could have dreamed of, in addition to the millions of books and materials of yesteryear. Let's use them all to their fullest potential. They're here for a reason, and that reason is to improve the way we think and communicate with the world.

Since there are so many genres and types of writing that you can choose to create, this guide will not focus on areas like character development, settings, and conflict. There are many online and workshop resources that you can easily seek out for the specific aspects of the  who, what, where, when, and whys of writing. Rather, this guide is for the technical aspects of your writing: the specifics that those websites and workshops don't get into like relevance, changing writing landscapes, and social media's importance to your book.

So whether you've written a book and are looking for some extra tips to make it shine, have writer's block and are looking for some ways to stay creative, or are ready to take the plunge and finally wrote your masterpiece, this book is for you.

The most important part of this book is to embrace your talents and to share them with the world. You are a writer. You were born a writer. I know, because I was born a writer too.

I can remember being a toddler and my father reading to me every night. I was amazed, and those stories stayed with me. I wanted to create my own. So I write.

I am a writer and proudly call myself one. Some writers are apprehensive of taking on this moniker, just as an artist often worries about labeling themselves as such. Do not fear the term 'writer.' Embrace it.

Pleased to Meet You

Hello, my name is Morissa. I despise ugly words like hankering, stank, frumpy, and robust, while words like eloquent, eccentric, metamorphosis, periphery, and anachronism make me beam.

The bio on my website[1] says I was pegged a literary prodigy, because I started reading, writing, and getting published at a very young age. I published my first book in high school and had my first bestseller while in college. It never felt like a "big deal" though. Writing was just what I loved to do, just like I enjoyed singing, dancing, and arts & crafts.

I think that's true for any writer: to be successful you have to enjoy it. Sure there are "rules" to follow (which is why guides like this are so helpful), just as there are "rules" to learning to play guitar or to paint well. It's all about using technique to channel your creativity and have fun. I wrote this guide to get you

---

[1] MorissaSchwartz.com

thinking about your own writing and to help you to be as successful as possible with sharing your voice and message with the world.

Five Reasons to Write

In case you need any extra motivation as to WHY you should write, here is some motivation.

1. You will grow through writing. You learn about yourself and the world just through jotting down your own ideas.

2. Writing is good for you. Honest! Studies have proven the benefits of writing on your health, from the ability to relax you to the spreading of feelings. It does wonders for you.

3. You can impact someone else who really needs it through your writing. Sometimes just seeing our own thoughts in writing can make a big difference to an individual.

4. Knowing that you produced something is a great feeling that comes from writing something. Creating content creates pride.

5. Writing can transform the world. It is the best way to express yourself in a way that will get through to others. Think about works that have impacted

Morissa Schwartz

you. They were all written by someone who shaped you. You can do the same.

James Grippando once said, "Until you understand why you write, you'll have a hard time figuring out who you are as a writer." That's why it's important you discover your voice. Your voice may change and evolve as you yourself do, but the brain behind it will remain definitive. This involves discovering what makes you who you are and what inspires you to write what you do.

To get started, here are some critical prompts you should answer before diving into your writing. They will help clear up many questions or issues that may arise when you write:

- *Who* do you want to be in your writing?

    Your voice as a writer is a very special one. Just as you can be anyone in life, your writing can be anything you want as well. You must shape an identity and personality for your writing. Of course, it can evolve and change overtime, but just as you are always you, your writer's voice is its own entity.

    - Example: My voice is one of positivity and honesty. I enjoy sharing my personal experiences and the stories of those who inspire me in the hopes that I may make an impact on my readers. And adding a little humor to my work is always fun.

- *What* drives you to have your voice heard?

    You should understand your motivational force. Figuring out why writing is important to you can help you to appreciate exactly what you have to say that will encourage others to respond to what you write.

- o Example: I want to bring happiness to the world. I believe that happiness the key to life, what we all strive for. If my writing can bring my readers joy, I have done my job.

- *Where* does your motivation lie?

There is a reason we write. Intrinsic and external. Discover and share the ones that are most important to you.

  - Example: I like the feeling I get when I write. It is when I am most at peace and like I am making a difference to my readers. My hope is that readers can share in my enthusiasm.

- *When* do you feel most comfortable?

This is more of a personality question that will help you decide the best time and place to write. When you are comfortable writing, your flow will be greatly improved.

  - o Example: I feel most comfortable at night, writing in my notebook, knowing that the whole world is asleep and that it is only me and my thoughts alone.

- *Why* do you write?

This is the biggest and most difficult question which may take a lot of time to discover. But once you find your definitive writing purpose, there is no stopping you.

- Example: I write, because I want to make a better future, not just for myself, but for the world.
- Better yet, here's an example from George Orwell: "When I sit down to write a book, I do not say to myself, 'I am going to produce a work of art.' I write it because there is some lie that I want to expose, some fact to which I want to draw attention, and my initial concern is to get a hearing."

When you can answer these questions, you are on the right road to unleashing your inner super writer.

Morissa Schwartz

The Times are Always A-Changin'

Apple coined, "Think different." Ignoring the irksome grammatical infraction of this statement, the sentiment is true for our generation. Our brains are wired differently than previous generations, thanks to our vast amounts of technology and how we now process the world around us.

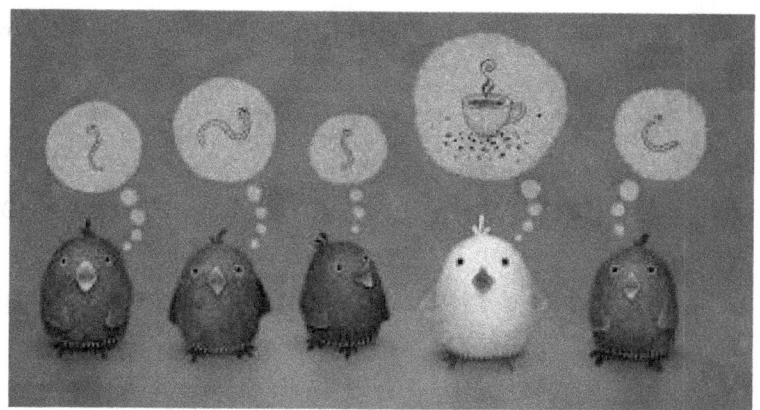

This has been proven by numerous scientific studies. Language is a reflection of our thought process, so of course, writing has seen a more measurable difference from past generations.

Writing has changed. A lot.

I still remember reading my tween magazines, like *Discovery Girls* and *Teen Ink*, where they had articles about the future of our language. This was when text-lingo was just going mainstream, and adults still didn't know what to make of it. The articles included how abbreviations we were using, from LOL to G2G, were impacting how we communicated. While many of those who grew up in generations past thought that our language was being 'dumbed down,' we knew we were simply revolutionizing it.

Just as the way each of us writes changes as we learn, grow, and improve, language changes. That's why Shakespearean language can seem so foreign. Clunky old-timey phrases get phased out and replaced with new, sleeker ones. Carpe Diem becomes YOLO. Language is ever-evolving.

In an interview with NPR, Paul McCartney spoke about how when his father heard the Beatles singing, "She loves you yeah, yeah, yeah..." he requested they sing "She loves you, yes, yes, yes"[2] instead, because there was a time when the word "yeah," that we use in everyday conversation without thought today, was reserved only as a slang word. Don't believe me? Ask your grandfather. This is just another example of how rapidly our language changes. New words become

---

[2] http://www.npr.org/2012/03/29/148609721/paul-mccartney-blows-kisses-to-his-fathers-era

common vernacular all the time. That's why the dictionary comes out with another edition every year.

A fun little factoid about the word slang: did you ever wonder where that word comes from? Slang stands for "shortened language." Again, slang is often thought of in a negative context, but what is so wrong with creating a smoother dialect? This is how language progresses.

We are the new generation of writing, eager to present fresh language to the world. We can use our vernacular to shape and frame the groundbreaking ideals of our time. Let's add some new words to the dictionary.

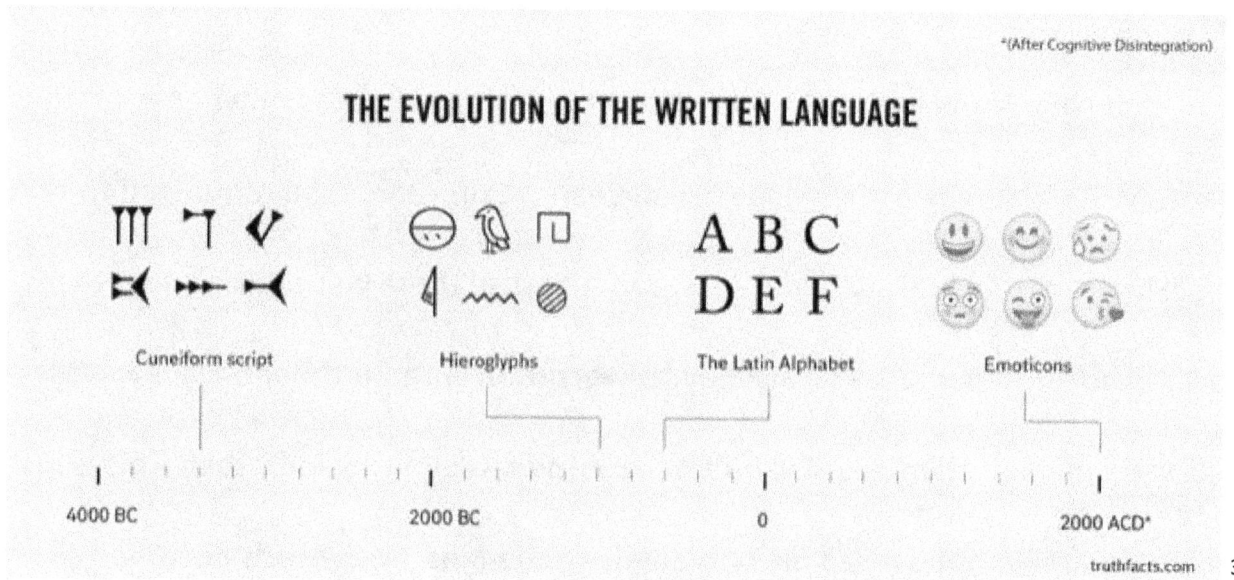

---

[3] Truthfacts.com

This is not necessarily a 'bad' thing. Language changes. Emojis are part of our evolution, as an image can be the sum of ideas. It works when we do it right. I am not saying to put emojis on your book (unless you think that could actually be pulled off...it's actually not such a 'crazy' idea). What I am saying is not to limit yourself. Explore and try something never before done before.

Morissa Schwartz

Write, Alright?

When you put thought and effort into your writing, you can be sure that it will make an impact. *Meliorism* is the belief that the world gets better, that humans can improve the world. Let's be the generation that does that. And you can do your part by making your writing something special to inspire people.

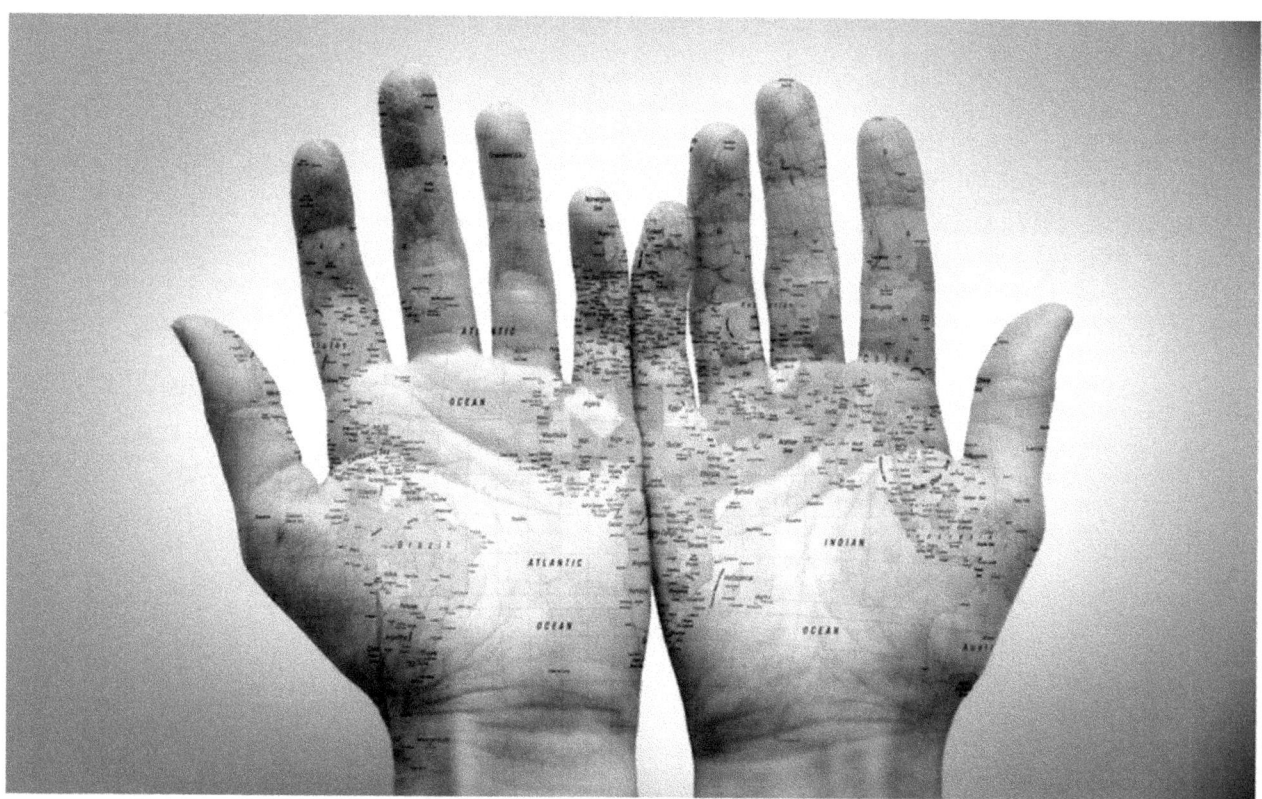

According to The Devil's Dictionary,[4] which is a hilarious dictionary with *honest* definitions of words (that you'll definitely want to read for creative writing inspiration and for a good laugh), the future is defined as *a time when affairs prosper, friends are true, and happiness is assured.* The beauty of this sarcastic

---
[4] http://www.thedevilsdictionary.com/

sentiment is the point that it is making: the *future* is not some utopia. We have now, and only now, to live our best lives and to follow our dreams. And by doing so, the future will shape up to be a better place. So if you want to write, write. If you want to use that writing to change the world, do it. This is your time, and tomorrow will be too, if you start with today.

Some say to write like no one is reading, but you also have an audience to write for. That is why my key is to always write what I would want to read.

When I was a child, I thought good writing was all about using big words. *The bigger the words the better the writing,* I thought. That's a common misconception, and it couldn't be farther from the truth. While challenging words can be fun and add to your writing, they are far from the epitome of good writing. What makes writing compelling and worthy of reading is the picture it paints. That is why I say, being thoughtful in your descriptions is the true determinate for good writing. Give your readers a clear image, and you've done your job as a successful writer.

Morissa Schwartz

Sustained Silent Reading Time

If you want to become an expert at anything, what do you do? You study. You practice. Writing is no different. You must read to write. It's as Stephen King said, "If you want to be a writer, you must do two things above all others: read a lot and write a lot."

You're off to a good start by reading this right now. Gold star for you!

Just remember: there is no such thing as too much reading. Read as much as your eyes will let you, and your brain will thank you for it. I'm not making that up. Reading has huge benefits. You can read more about them <u>on Life Hack</u>[5]. Yes, you read that right. Simply reading is considered a life hack because of all its benefits. Reading teaches you to think. Thinking is the first step to good writing. A professor of mine used to say that writing reflects the quality of your thinking, so if you write well, it is a good indication of your thought process.

Samuel Johnson once said, "The greatest part of a writer's time is spent in reading, in order to write; a man will turn over half a library to make one book." It's the truth, and I cannot stress it enough, you must read to write. You may also

---

[5] Http://www.lifehack.org/articles/productivity/when-you-start-read-more-these-10-things-will-happen.html?ref=fbp&n=2

notice many quotes used in this book. That is the product of reading. When you read, you create an arsenal of knowledge (sometimes in the form of quotes) to keep so that you can always be sure to express yourself in the best way possible.

With our mindboggling amounts tech, from smart phones to Netflix to the limitless Internet, you would assume that people read less books. But actually, twice as many people today read regularly than did in 1960.[6] That's a lot of reading. And that's a great thing. Reading is one of the most fun and rewarding activities there is. Not only is it exercise for the mind and spirit, but the thoughts we put on paper can shape the world. Just ask any great world leader past or present.

And if you think people aren't reading real books anymore, that couldn't be farther from the truth either. Book buying levels are at an all-time high, and not just e-books. According to MentalFloss[7], the popularity of eBooks have made people want hardcopy books even more. They appreciate the fact that they have options when it comes to choosing a book. I know, personally, reading is a very

---

[6] https://www.census.gov/population/socdemo/education/p23-08.pdf
[7] http://mentalfloss.com/article/63664/17-behind-scenes-secrets-bookstores

different experience between my iPad, my kindle, and a hardcover book, so I often vary which I read with. It all depends on my mood.

There are many classics and very popular books you won't want to miss. Ventucators[8] created a hilarious and fun video parody of "Uptown Funk" about many of greatest books, so check that out for a good laugh and take notes on the books you want to read…or the ones you haven't picked up since you were assigned them in class and may want to rediscover.

You should also be sure to check out books and writings by other young and innovative writers. See their styles and their voices, and use it to decide how you could write similar material. There are an infinite amount of books, with new ones released every day, so read, read, read…I promise you will never tire of it.

---

[8] https://www.youtube.com/watch?v=J6zclFUvdJ0

Get Creative

I invented a new word: plagiarism. I define plagiarism as the opposite of being creative, and being creative is what you should always strive to be. It is creativity that invents new technology, improves the world, and what will always set you apart.

Being creative is also good exercise for writing. You won't get writer's block if you keep working your mind muscles. Creativity comes in many forms. Some people draw. Some walk and explore. Some people daydream. The options are endless, and they can all better connect you with writing.

My personal favorite way to stay creative comes in the form of my neon green notebook. I keep lists of my favorite words and phrases in it, as well as interesting quotes and facts. I also collect my favorite images from magazines and old photos and paste them besides my words. That way whenever I'm feeling stuck, I just open my notebook and something always strikes my fancy. Then, I blog about it.[9]

---
[9] MyNeonGreenNotebook.blogspot.com

Morissa Schwartz

Writing is a very personal process. You will get to know yourself better than ever before. That is why exploring your mind and breaking through its barriers are crucial.

Writing prompts are also a great way to get your writer's mind working hard. I keep my favorites in my notebook and use them when I feel like creative writing. Most have elements of learning about yourself while also relating to society at large.

None have simple answers. Here are some of my personal favorites to get you thinking:

- What would you do if you could travel twenty years into your own future and live there for one day?
    - This can be about your ideal self, your predicted self, or even the future in general. Just keep writing.
- It started out as an unusual Monday morning, when...
    - This can be fictitious (sounds like a good sci-fi start) or even an odd memory you have.
- What would people say about me at my funeral?
    - While this may seem morbid at first glance, it is really an exploration of yourself and what you would want to be remembered for. What traits do you desire? How will you make a difference?
- What stands between me and complete happiness?
    - When we answer this, we often find that life is a lot simpler than it seems.
- The biggest issue that plagues society is...
    - This may get political or it could be an exploration of the issues you personally face daily and how you would want to change them.
- How old would I be if I didn't know my age? Why?

- People often called me mature as a child, an old soul. So I know my age would be much older than I actually am. Most of us do not quite fit mentally with our actual birth age. This is another question which delves into the realms of what makes you who you are.

- What sounds/scents do I love? Describe them.

    - Sounds and smells are among the hardest to describe. Really challenge yourself with this one so a reader would be able to hear/smell what you are describing in their head.

- What era/decade would I most like to live?

    - Maybe you can set a book in that time.

- Who would I want to trade lives with?

    - It's common knowledge that 'the grass is always greener,' so consider what it would be like to actually live someone else's life.

- If my life were a book/movie, what would be the title?

    - This question is a lot tougher than it looks, because it requires condensing your whole existence into a tiny title. It's like the Six Word Memoirs[10] that have been challenging writers for years.

---

[10] http://www.sixwordmemoirs.com/

- What is my biggest pet peeve? Why?

    o Writing is often reminiscent. Even recalling unpleasant memories can often wield some major results.

- If the whole world were listening, what would I say?

    o This question gets to the root of what is most important to you and what you think everyone else should know. You can write a lot on this topic.

- Write yourself a theme song.

    o A lighter prompt, this is also a fun way to sum up what makes you who you are by condensing yourself into a simple form.

- What is my most played song? Why?

    o Songs can remind us of other times, and the music we listen to has been scientifically proven to be very telling of our personalities. Explore this.

- What invention would the world be better without?

    o Most of the time we think of inventions as progress for society, but people always find drawbacks to new technology. See if you can think of these and how you would improve them.

Marcel Proust also compiled 35 of his own <u>questions</u>[11] that writers have been using through the years. Check them out to keep your mind moving.

Now, see if you can create some of your own prompts by thinking of creative situations, dreams, or questions you never thought of answering. You can use these experiences to write your best creative materials. As Dory would say, "just keep writing; just keep writing…" Write whenever you can, and you will surely be proud of the results.

Challenge yourself with your creativity. In 1939, Ernest Vincent Wright wrote *Gadsby*, a full-length novel without using the letter e, a single time. Just look at any sentence in this book, and see how prominent e is in the English language. Can you imagine what a creative challenge it must have been to think up all those other words for his book that did not include e? This is a perfect example of obsessive (in a good way) creativity. You can bet that writing that book must have been the most difficult thing for Mr. Wright, but the final result was a work of art, something completely new that had never been done before and that has inspired generations of writers for decades.

---

[11] http://thewritepractice.com/proust-questionnaire/

Actively writing isn't the only way to get your mind working, though. The idea for *Harry Potter* came to J.K. Rowling while she was riding a train. She didn't have a pen handy, so she let her mind wander and explore for hours before penning a single word. That allowed her creativity to skyrocket, and when she finally wrote it down, her thoughts were all there. Case and point: daydreaming is not a bad thing, kids.

Morissa Schwartz

Be Not Afraid

So many people will tell you that you MUST draw your readers in with that perfect first like. They'll say that you must write at least 500 words a day. People will tell you that if you don't diagram your book, it will fail. Yet, just like a zebra's stripes, we are all different. Maybe having a jaw-dropping first line won't matter so much because of the descriptive story you tell so well. Or perhaps you write in spurts and may write only 200 words one day and a whopping 2,000 the next. You could also be the type that writes your draft, then rewrites, edits, then rewrites, and does your best work during the editing stages. Whatever your process is, own it. That is yours. Do not stress over doing what others tell you works best for them. Find what works best for you, and go with it.

George R.R. Martin describes there being two different types of writers: architects and planters. He describes how architects will spend their energy drafting and writing from there while planters will place many seeds and see what grows. For that reason, there is no set way you should force yourself to write. If you do a little of both, that is fine. Just embrace your writing and let your ideas flourish however you may plan or cultivate them.

And when you do write, know who your audience is, and do not be afraid of your reader. As long as you put the time and effort in to make your writing shine, your readers will follow it. Chuck Palahniuk is one of my favorite authors (yes, he's the guy who wrote *Fight Club* and dozens of other brilliant works.) He put it best when he wrote, "Your audience is smarter than you imagine...younger readers distain most books – not because those readers are dumber than past readers, but because today's reader is smarter. Movies have made us very sophisticated about storytelling. And your audience is much harder to shock than you can ever imagine." [12] Palahniuk shocks audiences. He plays with reality, by distorting characters, time, and of course his language. Even someone who reads as much as me enjoys rereading his sentences and catching what I missed, because he dares me to. I welcome it. That is why you must challenge not only yourself but your readers as well. It makes the story and reading process so much more interesting.

But this advice comes with a warning, because this is not your ticket to write vaguely. Do not assume your reader will follow everything you write just because you wrote it. Writing as Palahniuk suggests includes writing with intent.

---

[12] https://litreactor.com/essays/chuck-palahniuk/stocking-stuffers-13-writing-tips-from-chuck-palahniuk

Morissa Schwartz

So read it back to yourself with a fresh mind, a reader's mind, and make sure that you will challenge them the right way.

The words you use can make all the difference to how your reader understands what you write. There are many ways to write one idea, but less to write it in an impactful way. This feelings wheel has been used in psychiatry for years, but getting into your characters requires getting into their imaginary heads so that your readers can and describing them as such.

This chart is a handy way to describe feelings. It was originally used as a psychology tool, but it can really help you to get into your characters' (and readers') minds while also helping you to step away from using the same old tired phrases. This will allow you to challenge readers.

Grammar Rules!

932 words break the I before E rule. Only 44 <u>follow it</u>[13]. That's just one of many examples of how difficult the English language can be.

The past, present, and future walked into a bar. It was tense. Tense can be the difference between a good writer and a great writer. As a writer, you're also expected to know the difference between *there, their, and they're* without flinching. You will need to properly use an adverb, and yes, that means you'll need to know what exactly an adverb is. At the same time, if you're still getting stuck on whether it is *a lot* or *alot,* just what constitutes a conjunction, or just need a quick refresher on language rules, peruse <u>these FAQs.</u>[14] It helps. I promise.

Oh, and embrace the <u>Oxford comma.</u>[15]

Something else that even the best writers get stuck on is which prepositions to use with adjectives. Use this handy chart from <u>Cork English Teacher</u>[16] as a reminder while you get started.

---

[13] http://myneongreennotebook.blogspot.com/2015/06/i-before-e.html
[14] http://drgrammar.org/frequently-asked-questions
[15] http://thewritepractice.com/why-you-need-to-be-using-oxford-commas/
[16] https://www.facebook.com/C.EnglishTeacher

adjective + preposition

accustomed to	comfortable with/in	fascinated by	limited to	sensitive to/about
accused of	connected with/to	fed up with	lucky at/with	serious about
addicted to	conscious of	free of/from	mad at/about	sick of
afraid of	content with	frightened of	married to	similar to
angry about/with	crazy about	friendly with	nervous of/about	shocked by
annoyed about/with/at	cruel to	fond of	notorious for	skilful at
allergic to	crowded with	furious about	opposed to	slow at
amazed at/by	cruel to	furnished with	optimistic about	sorry for/about
anxious about/to	curious about	full of	patient with	successful at/in
appreciated for	doubtful about	generous with	pessimistic about	suitable for
ashamed of	delighted at/about	guilty of/about	pleased with	sure of/about
associated with	derived from	gentle with	polite to	superior to
astonished at/by	different from	good at	popular with	surprised at/by
attached to	disappointed with	grateful to	presented with	suspicious of
aware of	eager for	happy about	proud of	sympathetic with
bad at	eligible for	hopeful of/about	punished for	talented at
based on	enthusiastic about	identical to	puzzled by/about	terrible at
beneficial to	excellent at	immune to	qualified for	terrified of
bored with	excited about	impressed with	ready for	tired of
brilliant at	experienced in	inferior to	related to	thankful to/for
busy with	exposed to	indifferent to	responsible for	typical of
capable of	envious of	jealous of	sad about	upset about
careful with/about/of	faithful to	kind to	safe from	used to
certain about	familiar with	keen on	satisfied with	wrong about/with
clever at/about	famous for	late for/to	scared of	worried about

CORK ENGLISH TEACHER

If this is all a bit overwhelming and music is more your speed, you may also want to revisit the School House Rock videos[17]. I promise they are not just for kids. They're nostalgic, catchy, and most importantly very educational if you need

---

[17] http://www.vrml.k12.la.us/curriculum/schoolhouserock/language_shr.htm

a grammar refresher or if you just want a song stuck in your head for a while. And then check out Robot Chicken's Satire [18] on it for a good laugh.

And if the word "irregardless" hurts your ears, you are easily annoyed by unnecessary commas, and you often find yourself silently (or sometimes not so silently) correcting other people's grammar, then congratulations! You're already a *grammar nerd.* And you're in company. Weird Al[19] is too, and he hilariously put all our thoughts into his song "Word Crimes." And if you prefer a life of memes, check out this take on our very real struggles of word nerds from the lovely folks at BuzzFeed.[20]

---

[18] https://www.youtube.com/watch?t=45&v=qCaZs6sYTa8
[19] https://www.youtube.com/watch?v=8Gv0H-vPoDc
[20] http://www.buzzfeed.com/jarrylee/faces-every-grammar-nerd-will-recognize#.ni4bm9aDDw

So, But, and...And

Your teachers probably told you to never start a sentence with 'but' or 'so,' right? They were right...and wrong.

When you are writing a professional essay, of course, you must not write as you speak. Keep it professional. However, when writing your own fiction or creative non-fiction, one of the most important keys to resonating with readers is allowing them to hear your voice. So, you don't want to sound like a robot. You want to sound like you. Using words like *and, so,* and *but* (AKA conjunctions) at the start of your sentence can give your writing a little personality. Just don't overdo it.

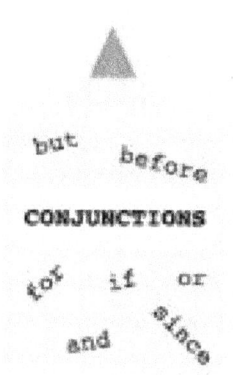

You were taught a lot of grammar rules in school, and as Business Insider[21] puts it, many of them were *white lies.* Meaning, that when your teacher taught you not to start a sentence with a conjunction, he or she was trying to teach you un-fragmented writing, but that doesn't mean that you have to write that way all the time. In fact, using conjunctions in that way can often make your writing more varied and colorful.

---

[21] http://www.businessinsider.com.au/harvard-steven-pinker-debunks-10-grammar-myths-2015-8

So don't be afraid to start a sentence in your book with 'but.' Your readers need to relate to your voice, and writing conversationally can be a great way to do this.

Morissa Schwartz

Be Concise, B-E Concise

Mark Twain once wrote in a note, "I wanted to write you a shorter letter, but I didn't have the time." It takes effort to be concise. It takes time, patience, and most importantly, editing.

Being concise means you say everything you want in a more packable way. Of course, this means you'll want to use run-on sentences sparingly. But more than that, being concise in your writing makes it easier for readers to understand. Plus, it sounds much better and challenges you to write more clearly.

The brain needs breaks when reading. Periods give them that.

I would compare this to your favorite online article a la *Buzzfeed, Hello Giggles,* or *Cracked*. They are not overwhelmingly long. They give you the information you need in a fun way that you're likely to share with others. While it takes you minimal effort to read and enjoy those articles, you can bet it takes time to write those posts.

I have written a lot of articles for *Entertainment Weekly's Community.* The most challenging part is keeping them under 500 words. I often draft a post about something like *South Park* or *A Clockwork Orange* at about 2,000 words and then have to chop, chop, chop. And you know what? The 500 word article is always way better than the 2,000 word one. There is no fluff. It's smooth. That's what makes readers want to read your work.

Easier said than done, which is why when Stephen King says, "When your story is ready for rewrite, cut it to the bone. Get rid of every ounce of excess fat. This is going to hurt; revising a story down to the bare essentials is always a little like murdering children, but it must be done," it's more than true.

Write with purpose. A great Hunter S. Thompson quote says, "Not a wasted word. This has been a main point to my literary thinking all my life," and this is a very helpful sentiment. You want to be sure that your words resonate with readers. Choose your words carefully and make it tight. If you do that, writing and varying your wording gets easier. It's easier if you do this step as early as the first draft, meaning you think carefully before drafting, but again everyone is different, so if you are confident you can remove the excess wording in the editing stages, go for it!

You will want to vary your sentence lengths. There's nothing worse than reading a bunch of short sentences in a row (which becomes monotonous) or multiple compound sentences in a row (which becomes overwhelming.) You will want a few short sentences followed by a longer sentence. That is what keeps your writing interesting. Gary Provost was one of the great writers of the twentieth century, and he summed up using varying sentence lengths in this easily digestible quote, "This sentence has five words. Here are five more words. Five-word sentences are fine. But several together become monotonous. Listen to what is happening. The writing is getting boring. The sound of it drones. It's like a stuck record. The ear demands some variety. Now listen. I vary the sentence length, and I create music. Music. The writing sings. It has a pleasant rhythm, a lilt, a harmony. I use short sentences. And I use sentences of medium length. And sometimes, when I am certain the reader is rested, I will engage him with a sentence of considerable length, a sentence that burns with energy and builds with all the impetus of a crescendo, the roll of the drums, the crash of the cymbals–sounds that say listen to this, it is important."[22]

At the same time though, play around with your language. You never know what you will get, I wrote the following, admittedly very strange story by using exclusively one-syllable words. It gives a dark story a very childlike feel in this case, and using language in this manner can make your writing something different, or at the very least, get you thinking differently. I realized that I often use words like "almost," "every," and "little." I had to find synonyms or delete these words completely for this to work. Exercises like this can help expand your vocabulary and how you vary your usage. This is my monosyllable story:

'When I went to the mall with Jen and Jack, we saw an odd sight. There was a cat who walked on two legs like he was a real man. Could he have been a real man? No. His long fur showed that he was a real cat. He purred and hissed.

We did not know how he got to the mall in the first place. We knew he could not drive in. And to walk all that way on two paws would be hard.

We tried not to stare, but we still did. What an odd sight.

---

[22] Gary Provost

Morissa Schwartz

I was young, not yet a teen, a girl of twelve, so I did not doubt what I saw. None of us did.

The cat walked with a girl who wore her red hair in a bun, and her long black dress flowed with each step. She seemed to be the same age as my aunt: not quite as old as my mom but not a kid like me.

Then, the black cat went in the Gap. The girl followed as they strolled.

He looked at the spring shirts. The girl picked up a lime one, and the cat hissed. Then, a blue one. The cat growled. Last, she showed him a gray one and the cat purred. It was a small kid's size. They got pants to match.

The girl pulled out some bills and bought him the clothes at the front. The clerk's mouth was open wide as she rang them up, but she did not say a word. I guess she did not want to be rude.

The girl put the shirt on the cat as he raised his arms and put a paw through each sleeve. And then the pants went on one leg at a time.

He showed off to the girl.

"You look good," she said as she took his paw in her hand and off they went. They whizzed right past us, in the way of the pet store. We felt their breeze as they walked fast and were soon out of sight.

What were they up to?

Jen said we should go to the pet shop to see what was up. I did not want to walk that far. And yes, I feared the cat just a bit.

I said, "Let's just stay here." Jack called me a scared slug. I had to prove him wrong.

So I lead the way as my friends and I went toward the pet store. It was quite far from the Gap in the next wing. We walked past Bass, The Loft, Claires, and then Champs at a fast pace and did not speak a word. But our brains were not still as we thought of the weird black cat.

"This way," Jen said. We turned left by Clarks, Wet Seal, Coach, Pink, Lids, Sprint, and then we saw the pet shop.

We marched toward the big red sign, marked *Crab Tree Mall Pet Shop,* and in we went.

I did not think we would see a sight more strange than the cat. But we did.

A small man on all fours, his hands and feet on the ground, stood in a cage like a cat. But he was a real man.

That is when I knew that the cat and the man must have switched. Now it all made sense. Sort of.

Jen was right. The red haired girl and the cat on two legs were there. They stared at the man.

"You did this to me," the man's eyes were red. He yelled at the girl from the cage, as he thrashed against the steel frame.

The girl shushed him. He yelled more.

The girl took out a wood stick from her side and said for him to stop. He did as soon as the wand came out. He did not speak another word.

"The girl must be a witch," I said to Jack and Jen.

Jen's eyes grew bright, "A witch? A real witch? Like the Queen from *Snow White*? Or Prue from *Charmed*? Or Meg from *Meg and Mog*?"

"Sure," I said, not sure what Jen was up to.

With that, Jen walked to the girl and plopped on her hands and knees. *Oh, no.*

"Me next!" Jen said as the red haired witch took out her wand. She swung it in the air, said a short spell, and Jen grew a tail.

That was the day I lost my best friend. But at least I got a new pet.'

Morissa Schwartz

Very

Would you rather be known as a very good writer or an eloquent writer?

"Very" diminishes your words. Avoid using it. You can always use a more powerful word. Don't write that someone is 'very happy.' Say they are 'ecstatic.' Do you see how much better that sounds?

Here's a great handy chart from *Writers Write* that can help when you feel stuck in a 'very' rut.

45 Ways to avoid using the word 'very'			
Avoid saying very:	Rather say:	Avoid saying very:	Rather say:
afraid	terrified	neat	immaculate
angry	furious	old	ancient
bad	atrocious	poor	destitute
beautiful	exquisite	pretty	beautiful
big	immense	quiet	silent
bright	dazzling	risky	perilous
capable	accomplished	roomy	spacious
clean	spotless	rude	vulgar
clever	brilliant	serious	solemn
cold	freezing	small	tiny
conventional	conservative	strong	unyielding
dirty	squalid	stupid	idiotic
dry	parched	tasty	delicious
eager	keen	thin	gaunt
fast	quick	tired	exhausted
fierce	ferocious	ugly	hideous
good	superb	valuable	precious
happy	jubilant	weak	feeble
hot	scalding	wet	soaked
hungry	ravenous	wicked	villainous
large	colossal	wise	sagacious
lively	vivacious	worried	anxious
loved	adored		
www.writerswrite.co.za			

And while we're on the subject of being mindful of your language...

Vary Your Language

Did you ever notice how saying "a mile a minute" sounds a lot faster than saying, "Sixty miles per hour?" The words you use can change how a reader responds to your writing. You always want to *show* your readers, not *tell* them. This means instead of writing something like, "Sarah was sad," you write something like, "Sarah's head was down as a tear fell from her left eye." Do you see how sentence two paints a more complete picture of Sarah's sadness without even saying the word *sad*? For a more illustrated example, check out this handy example.[23]

You want to stand out, right? Well, your writing should be the same way. That is why, instead of using 'boring' words, like *good, big,* or *said* all the time, you should enrich your vocabulary.

Test it out the next time you're texting. Instead of writing 'haha' for the thousandth time, try "how jocular" or that you found that particular joke "cachinnating." It may not be as convenient as LOL and may make your friends scratch their heads, but it is a fun word-varying exercise that will get you in the groove of looking for new ways to say old things.

---

[23] http://editing.xterraweb.com/writing-tips/showing-vs-telling-write-with-the-five-senses

Said in particular is a word that gets overused. "She said." "He said." "They said." Yawn. Let's spice it up! "She exclaimed." "He murmured." "They lamented." See the difference? Again, this is about painting a picture in your readers' minds. Colorful language is key to leaving a lasting impression with your readers.

You can see some more examples of words you should avoid using too often and some suggestions here.[24]

One of my favorite tools for finding exciting words is the Visual Thesaurus.[25] With it, not only will you find more exciting vernacular, but you can be sure you're using them correctly. Vocab Grabber[26] is also a great tool to use if you want to learn a word and remember its meaning and usage.

---

[24] http://justenglish.me/2014/11/06/18-common-words-that-you-should-replace-in-your-writing/
[25] https://www.visualthesaurus.com/
[26] http://www.visualthesaurus.com/vocabgrabber/

Writing for the New Generation

Alternatives for Top 30 Overused Words

A lot:	copious, myriad, several, plentiful, countless, numerous.
Amazing/Awesome:	fascinating, incredible, wonderful, stunning, marvellous, astonishing.
Also:	in addition to, besides, moreover, as well as, furthermore, additionally.
Bad:	deficient, inferior, dreadful, atrocious, unacceptable, dissatisfactory, erroneous.
Big:	considerable, vast, colossal, extensive, substantial, immense, ample, copious.
Change:	transform, modify, revise, switch, transition, adjust, alter, rework.
Definitely:	absolutely, undeniably, positively, doubtless, plainly, surely, specifically.
Easy:	uncomplicated, effortless, straightforward, adept, amiable, responsive.
Fine:	outstanding, exceptional, magnificent, well-made, admirable, first-rate.
Get:	acquire, obtain, accomplish, attain, extort, extract, glean, secure, procure.
Give:	bestow, relinquish, permit, award, bequeath, dispense, administer, contribute.
Good:	satisfying, stupendous, proficient, valuable, acceptable, worthy, congenial.
Great:	excellent, exceptional, first-rate, unmitigated, proficient, marvellous, expert.
Happy:	contented, jubilant, ecstatic, elated, overjoyed, captivated, upbeat, gratified.
Hard:	arduous, troublesome, demanding, strenuous, onerous, exacting, complicated.
Help:	advice, guidance, remedy, corrective, assist, service, assist, cooperation, comfort.
Important:	crucial, significant, essential, critical, meaningful, vital, far-reaching, imperative.
Interesting:	engaging, stimulating, captivating, compelling, absorbing, meaningful, notable.
Keep:	retain, preserve, possess, manage, amass, conserve, detain, garner, control.
Know:	experience, comprehend, be acquainted, distinguish, differentiate, realise, discern.
Like (adj):	similar, comparable, related, corresponding, equivalent, resembling, equal.
Like (verb):	enjoy, relish, admire, cherish, regard, extol, appreciate, commend, respect.
Look:	glimpse, contemplate, survey, inspection, glance, attention, glance, review.
Nice:	gracious, pleasurable, charming, amiable, well-mannered, genial, pleasing, seemly.
Quite:	considerably, absolutely, thoroughly, in all respects, utterly, all in all, purely.
Really:	literally, genuinely, categorically, in effect, unquestionably, undoubtedly, honestly.
Said:	announced, expressed, uttered, revealed, described, disclosed, divulged, intimated.
So:	apparently, accordingly, likewise, similarly, consequently, hence, provided that.
Then:	suddenly, formerly, in that event, subsequently, appropriately, as a consequence.
Very:	profoundly, extremely, truly, greatly, notably, prominently, suitably, immensely, vitally.

www.proofeditwrite.com

Write Mindfully

Just because you've heard a phrase many times, doesn't necessarily mean it's true. There are many examples of mindless phrases, clichés like "When in Rome" or "do as I say," that are so overused, we do not even think about their meanings anymore. That is why you should avoid them.

Elite Daily[27] goes into further detail about this phenomenon and describes why phrases like "I have no regrets" are regrettable. When everyone says a phrase like that, it is no longer special. When you write a phrase like that, your writing loses that special something. You become just another book on the shelf rather than the book that changed lives.

The same goes for clichés. I don't want to say you should avoid clichés like the plague, but you really shouldn't use them. You're writing is better than that. You owe it to yourself to stand out with your own words. There is a great list of phrases you should probably avoid on Be a Better Writer.[28]

Instead of saying something like "He was blind as a bat," a tired and overused cliché that adds nothing to your writing, find a way to demonstrate his inability to see through a sentence like, "He walked into the table and felt around

---

[27] http://elitedaily.com/life/culture/phrases-we-say/1086232/
[28] http://www.be-a-better-writer.com/cliches.html

for the door." I never said he was blind in that sentence, but you can infer it, while now having a picture of his actions. In the "blind as a bat" phrase, you don't

even know the level of his visual impairment, how it impacts him, or why you should care. But you do with the second sentence.

Morissa Schwartz

Using Rhetorical Devices

You don't want your writing to be boring or predictable. You want to shake your readers. Give them something unexpected. That is why rhetorical devices are so necessary.

By using something like an allegory to illustrate a point in a story, you better paint a clear picture for your reader. If you want to allow the reader to fully understand how important something is to the story, an exaggeration or hyperbole may be necessary.

There are *literally* dozens of these devices. Mental Floss[29] has a great list and explanations, where you can learn some of the different types and when they are best used.

Think of your words like a painting. You can illustrate them in any way. So make them colorful or make them bleak. It's up to you. The end product is what matters and what will be completely up to you.

---

[29] http://mentalfloss.com/article/60234/21-rhetorical-devices-explained

Editing and Proofreading

First off, never try to say the word *editing* aloud for the same reason that you should never say *clasps:* It is a very ugly word that will make you sound ridiculous every time. It's funny that they would make such an important word so awkward sounding. They really should have edited that word before putting it in the dictionary.

A lot of people will tell you editing is just as important as writing or that the real writing gets done when you edit. This is true and untrue. I find that during a first draft, the ideas are fresher and more imaginative. When editing, sure you can expand on them, but while writing your first draft, if all you're thinking is that you'll fix all this up in the editing stages, you're leaving yourself with a bit of a nightmare to take care of. So try your best in the first draft, and don't look to editing as your savior but as your polish. It's how you make your writing shine. So build on your writing with editing, but don't rely solely on it.

Morissa Schwartz

    Similar to editing, which focuses more on flow, readability, and building on your writing, proofreading is all about the grammar. Now you may think *easy peasey, I have spell check.* Sorry to break it to you, but the *Spelling and Grammar Check* are great on Word, but they don't cover readability of your work. While you should definitely have other people read over your work, you should perfect as much as you can on your own first. Flow is important. That is why I love the Hemingway App.[30] Just copy and paste your text into it online, and it evaluates your flow with reasoning behind it. This also helps in the long run, because you will see your errors and how to correct them. Then show your friends, so they can give you honest feedback without being distracted by glaring errirs and mystakes.

---

[30] http://www.hemingwayapp.com/

A Brief Break

This section will be a bit different from all the others. This is a short story I wrote, but will be a great example of how a story evolves. The first section will be my initial story. A simple story told through the main character, Thony, a patient at a psychiatrist's office based on a prompt I read that asked writers to create an odd character seeking help. My mind went on to create attentionspan-less Thony. But then, I wondered how this same story would turn out if it weren't focusing just on Thony, but making his psychiatrist, a basically faceless entity in the first version, the protagonist. And so Dr. White was born. The final and most complete version of this story focuses on both characters, evolving them and making them a bit more human, and goes in a completely different direction by the end. This is a great example of how a story or book can be very different from the time you begin writing until the time you end. You should never limit your creativity or stop writing. Explore.

That is how this story came about, from exploration. It was far from my comfort zone. For starters, I wrote non-fiction more than any other genre, and this is pure fiction. Second, both protagonists are part of an older generation than myself, dealing with problems that I have not had to. The setting is also foreign to me: I have never stepped foot into a therapist's office before. I also used a more

Morissa Schwartz

negative tone, while in most of my writing, I try to inspire readers with an upbeat tone. This story was a real challenge that I set for myself. However, through using my imagination and creativity, I was able to create a world around these characters. I submerged myself in is and really got to know both doctor and patient. That is what should happen when you write. Get so into it that it feels like a reality.

Version 1: *And How Does That Make You Feel?*

Thony tapped his bony fingers on his shaking leg as he looked around the therapist's waiting room. There were your standard clinical office items: a grimy fish tank with miniature placco and angel fish swimming at a glacial pace, old magazines with the good articles ripped out, and miniature pastel colored sunset paintings by an artist whose name would not be recognized by even the most celebrated of artistic scholars.

There was bouncy pop music playing on the waiting room television, the kind that Thony hated most. It was some boy band playing their new hit on *Live with Mikey and Kiley.* Mikey's big teeth bothered Thony almost as much as Kiley's whiny voice. She was worse than those Mickey Mouse Club kids.

"Mr. Alexander," the stout lady with a clipboard called. Thony was noodling on his phone, switching between apps.

She walked over to him, the only person in the waiting room, "Mr. Alexander?"

Thony stood up without looking at the woman and started towards the therapist's office. It was the first door on the left. "Dr. White" was written in white letters on the black slab that hung proudly in the center of the top of the door. Thony took a seat on the couch-bed hybrid. He didn't hear the stout lady say that his appointment would begin in a few minutes. He was too busy feeling around his pockets to make sure that his keys were still there. Once he located them, he pulled out his wallet. He looked at his platinum card, then his gym membership card, and then his Starbucks card.

"I wonder what the balance is on my account," he said aloud as he pulled out his iPhone 6 Plus. He had $26.74 left in his Starbucks Quick Pay App. It was almost time to reload. He wouldn't want to pay cash for his coffee. It takes too long to get exact change, and he hated carrying around quarters, dimes, and the dreaded penny that weighed down his pockets.

Dr. White waltzed in and took a seat on her chair in the center of the room.

"Th-ony? Am I pronouncing that correctly?" The doctor clicked her pen.

"Mhmm."

The doctor looked down at her clipboard, "So tell me why you're here, Mr. Alexander."

Thony barely waited for Dr. White to finish her sentence before he began yammering, "Well, I've been having trouble paying attention to what people say lately. You know, they say something, and it goes in one ear and right out the other. I just get so caught up in my own thoughts that anything anyone else has to say feels so insignificant. And then I end up not listening to them."

Thony paused and looked at Dr. White's Moleskin pen gliding back and forth.

Then he continued, "I'm a good guy, really. But I don't like not listening to people, because it makes me feel like I'm not a good guy. It makes me feel like some sort of narcissist. It makes me feel awful."

The doctor nodded as she admired the stick figure caricature that she had just finished. Her eyes were glazed over. She took a sip of her vente caramel macchiato as she asked, "And how does that make you feel?"

Morissa Schwartz

Version 2: *And How Does that Make Me Feel?*

Dr. White's 2:30 appointment was a no-show, but Dr. White wasn't complaining. The patient hadn't called ahead, so she would still get paid despite not actually seeing him. And her receptionist had called in sick, so she was the only one at the office. Dr. White took this time to ingest her second Quest Protein Bar of the day. She loved her protein bars almost as much as she enjoyed her espressos.

She looked over her planner. Dr. White was expecting a patient at 3:00. He was a new patient named Thony Alexander. She sat down at her Macbook Pro to check her Facebook feed.

"Aww, Stephanie's engaged," she smiled. She wondered if she'd be invited to the wedding. She and Stephanie hadn't actually spoken in a few years, but they kept in contact through social media. Dr. White knew she received more invitations than her less successful friends simply because she had *doctor* before her name.

After a few minutes clicking through photos of Stephanie, the ring, and her fiancé, who Dr. White couldn't help but find attractive, she brought herself to the waiting room. That's where she saw Thony sitting alone. He was seven minutes early.

She approached him, "Mr. Alexander?"

Thony stood up without looking at Dr. White. She could already tell she wouldn't like him, but she had to push those negative feelings aside to maintain a professional demeanor. She showed him to her office where Thony took a seat on the couch-bed hybrid.

She told him that his appointment would begin in a few minutes. She wasn't sure if he had heard her or now but didn't really care. Dr. White wanted to see if she could figure out how long Stephanie and her new fiancé had been in a relationship before getting engaged.

She went into the next room, and plopped down on her leather chair. She scrolled through Stephanie's feed to find that they had been in a relationship since May 2014.

"Seems a bit soon," she said quietly. After a couple of minutes, Dr. White pried herself from the computer screen. She was now three minutes late for her appointment with Thony.

Dr. White grabbed her clipboard, Moleskin pen, and vente caramel macchiato and headed in to see Thony.

She took a seat on her chair in the center of the room.

"Th-ony? Am I pronouncing that correctly?" Dr. White interrupted Thony's phone play.

"Mhmm," Thony answered.

Dr. White looked at her clipboard, "So tell me why you're here, Mr. Alexander." She was just going through the motions. All Dr. White could actually focus on was Stephanie, her fiancé, and that stupid diamond ring.

Thony began yammering," Well, I've been having trouble paying attention to what people…"

She tried to nod her head encouragingly as Thony spoke, but her thoughts began to shift almost immediately.

Why does Stephanie get a nice wedding? She barely got through college. But me, I'm a successful doctor. Where's my Mr. Right? Where's my happily ever after?

Dr. White admired the stick figure caricature of a bride and groom that she had just finished on her clipboard.

She took a sip of her vente caramel macchiato as she asked, "And how does that make you feel?"

Morissa Schwartz

Version 3: **Modern Therapy**

Dr. White's 2:30 appointment was a no-show, but she wasn't complaining. The patient hadn't given notice, so she would still get paid. Her receptionist called in sick, so she was the only one at the office. She liked it that way.

Dr. White ingested her second Quest Protein Bar of the day. At her last check-up, her doctor said that she was clinically overweight. She thought that the protein bars were a good substitute for her old standby: the Starbucks blueberry muffin. And once she lost her extra pounds, she had already planned to treat herself to the light version of the muffin to celebrate.

Dr. White slid her fingers through her frizzy dirty blonde hair as she looked over her leather bound planner. She was expecting a patient at 3:00. He was a new patient named Thony Alexander. *What kind of a stupid name is Thony? Was it actually "Tony" with an "h" accidentally added?* Dr. White double-checked the chart. She just couldn't imagine what kind of parents would name their kid "Thony."

"Thony," she said aloud and laughed. She couldn't say his name without sounding like she had a Cindy Brady lisp.

Since she had some spare time before her next appointment, she sat down at her Macbook Pro to check her Facebook feed. She enjoyed stalking Facebook friends almost as much as she loved chugging her espressos.

"Aww, Stephanie's engaged," She smiled a broken grin and wondered if she'd be invited to the wedding. She and Stephanie hadn't actually spoken in a few years, but they kept in contact through social media. Dr. White knew she received more invitations than her less successful friends simply because of the prestige that came with having *doctor* in her name.

Dr. White and Stephanie were friends from childhood. They lived on the same street and were close for a while. After school they'd play at Dr. White's house. She always had the newer toys. She was more privileged, as an only child, than Stephanie who had to share her stuff with two sisters.

In high school, Stephanie became more popular than Dr. White when she joined the girls' soccer team, even though she was just second string. Anyone who played sports was automatically afforded friends that academics like Dr. White were not.

When Dr. White became a therapist, she thought she had finally beaten Stephanie at life. She had a high-paying job, while Stephanie was just some PR person. But she was one-upped by this woman yet again.

After a few minutes of clicking through photos of Stephanie, the ring, and her fiancé, who Dr. White couldn't help but find attractive, she brought herself to the waiting room. That's where she saw Thony sitting alone. He was seven minutes early.

***

Thony tapped his bony fingers on his shaking leg as he looked around. There were your standard clinical office items: a grimy fish tank with miniature placco and angel fish swimming at a glacial pace, old magazines with the good articles ripped out, and miniature pastel colored sunset paintings by an artist whose name would not be recognized by even the most celebrated artistic scholars.

A boy band was performing their new bouncy pop music, the kind that Thony hated most, on a day-time talk show, which played on the waiting room television. It was just one click above a mute. But Thony could hear it, and it annoyed him. Until he saw the hosts. Kiley's whiny voice bothered him. She was worse than those Mickey Mouse Club kids.

***

Dr. White had learned how to tune the television out after all those years. Even the low quality, overacted local car commercials in which they are way too excited about nothing.

Dr. White approached him. "Th-ony? Am I pronouncing that correctly?"

"Mhmm," Thony stood up without looking at the doctor and started towards her office. It was the first door on the left. "Dr. White" was written in egg cream colored letters on the charcoal slab that hung proudly in the center of the door.

She thought he looked older than her, even though he was the same age: thirty-two. Maybe it was the dark circles under his eyes. Perhaps his job as a defense attorney left those stress marks. Surely, his children and wife contributed.

Dr. White could already tell she didn't like her new patient, but she had to maintain a professional demeanor. Her left eye twitched. She had convinced herself that her eye only twitched due to their dryness, not stress.

Morissa Schwartz

***

Thony took a seat on the couch-bed hybrid. Dr. White told him that his appointment would begin in a few minutes after she updated his files.

He hadn't heard her. He was too busy fiddling with a string on the bottom of his shirt. Once he got that situation taken care of by pulling at it until it snapped, he was able to sit calmly for a moment, before he began feeling around his pockets to make sure that his keys were still there. Once he located them, he pulled out his wallet. He looked at his platinum card, then his gym membership card, and then his Starbucks card.

"I wonder what the balance is on my account," he thought as he pulled out his iPhone 6 Plus. He had $26.74 left on his Starbucks Quick Pay App. It was almost time to reload. He wouldn't want to pay cash for his coffee. It took too long to get exact change, and he hated carrying around quarters, dimes, and the dreaded penny that weighed down his pockets.

***

In the other room, Dr. White thought about her own relationships or lack thereof. In high school, she never really dated. She was too preoccupied with her grades and achieving her dream of becoming a doctor. In college, she dated a philosophy major named Steve for a month, but she found out he was dating two other girls at the same time. She did not like games like that. She decided to put her career first and focus solely on that for a while.

By the time she was twenty-eight, and one of the only singles she knew, she decided to look for love again. She had the career that she had worked so hard for. Now it was time to have it all: the loving husband, the large house, the beautiful family.

She met a guy named George through a blind date. They were together fourteen months, but now she couldn't even utter his name. He just wouldn't commit: She mentioned moving in together; he said they should see other people. She asked why; he said she was too demanding. She called him an imbecile; they never spoke again.

Dr. White tried dating other guys, but none were right. Some were too dumb with no prospects. Others were lazy heathens. Many were just shallow and wrong. Those were her excuses anyway, especially when they never called her back.

She had grown colder as the years went on. Having her *dream job* meant nothing without the other parts of her life that were missing and keeping her life from being perfect.

She scrolled through Stephanie's feed to find that Stephanie and her new fiancé had been in a relationship since May 2013.

"Two years? Seems a bit soon," she muttered. Dr. White scrolled through some photos of the couple, took a few deep breaths, and pried herself from the screen. She was now three minutes late for her appointment with Thony. She didn't think he'd notice.

Dr. White grabbed her clipboard, Moleskin pen, and vente caramel macchiato. She took a seat on her chair in the center of the therapy room.

"So tell me why you're here, Thony."

Thony barely waited for Dr. White to finish her sentence before he began rambling. She tried to nod her head encouragingly as Thony spoke.

Why does Stephanie get a nice wedding? She barely got through college. But me, I'm a successful doctor. Where's my Mr. Right? Where's my happily ever after?

***

Thony let out a nervous cough.

"...And I've been having trouble paying attention to what people say lately. You know, they say something, and it goes in one ear and right out the other. I just get so caught up in my own thoughts that anything anyone else has to say feels so insignificant. And then I end up not listening to them."

Thony paused and looked at Dr. White's silver pen gliding back and forth. It looked expensive.

Then he continued, "I'm a good guy, really. But I don't like not listening to people, because it makes me feel like I'm not a good guy. It makes me feel like some sort of narcissist. It makes me feel awful."

Dr. White admired the stick figure caricature of a bride and groom that she had just finished on her clipboard. She took a sip of her creamy macchiato as she asked, "And how does that make you feel?"

Thony sighed. He decided to just keep talking. He enjoyed hearing the sound of his own voice. It was deep. He always thought he belonged on the radio.

***

Dr. White kept doodling and nodding. She was glad she didn't have to prod Thony to talk. Less work for her. Besides, he had a wife, a family, and a good job. Why couldn't he just appreciate it? Some people weren't so fortunate.

She gave her groom doodle a nice big mustache. Then, she added devil horns to the bride.

The two went through the therapist/patient motions a little while longer. Then, Dr. White's phone alarm went off. The session was over.

***

Thony went home to his wife and told her that his therapy was great. He assured her that he was all better and would never have to see a therapist again. Thony thought that therapists were for loonies with problems. His wife was the one who made him go to therapy after he forgot to pick his son up from school for the third time. She thought that a little head clearing was all he needed to get his mind back. When she went on to tell him about her day working in the daycare and how his son got an 76 on his spelling test, he nodded while he swiped blue jewels on his phone.

"That's nice, honey," he said.

***

After driving home to her luxury apartment in the suburbs, Dr. White's evening consisted of her sobbing into her phone for an emergency session with her own therapist, Dr. Chellovek. She needed to vent.

"It's not fair!" she yelled into the phone about her friend's engagement, "I just feel so alone."

There was silence on the other end of the line. Dr. Chellovek cleared his throat before saying, "And how does that make you feel?"

Dr. White's eye twitched as she dunked her Quest Bar in her espresso laced coffee, which spilled all over her computer. The lights emanating from the machine flickered on and off, until finally, the blue Facebook screen was replaced by a black one.

Dr. White gasped. Her body remained still as the coffee continued to drip on her computer. But her fingers never stopped moving as she quickly tapped the Facebook app on her phone. She stared longingly at Stephanie's engagement ring on the smaller screen.

"Lonely," she answered.

Morissa Schwartz

Book Length

Here is some good news and bad news. The typical novel about 100,000 words. YA isn't too much better coming in at a whopping 60,000 words. That's a lot of writing even for the most seasoned professional writer. But here's the good news: writing has no rules. Especially modern writing.

See, an eBook can be as short as you'd like. I wouldn't recommend a haiku of a book, but the point it, the length of your book is entirely up to you. eBooks are traditionally around 20,000 or more words, but don't imprison yourself by trying to just add or subtract words to meet a word count guide, especially since every genre and book is different. I see this tweet or ones similar way too often:

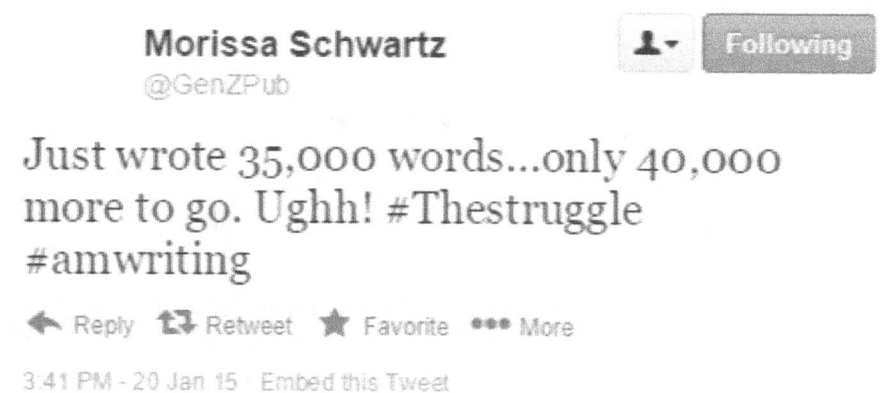

Doing this not only takes all the fun out of writing, but it take away your creativity. It makes writing feel like a chore. Guess what happens when you're not enjoying your writing? Its quality suffers. If you want to write well, don't limit yourself in any way. Especially with word count. This isn't Mrs. Smith's writing class where you have to change your font size to fit her page requirements. You're the boss of your own writing. Write as much or as little as you'd like. If it's enticing, people will read it and enjoy it, regardless of its length.

Doris Lessing once said, "There are no laws for the novel. There never have been, nor can there ever be." This is liberating, it may seem a little scary to know that whatever you can dream up can become a reality, but it is important to realize that no rule is set in writing. That is how innovative writing works. You do something that has never been done before or something in a new way, often through blatantly not following established rules. On that same note and to complete this idea, I bring you Jules Renard's rule that "Style is to forget all styles." That is why many musicians like Keith Richards do not like to classify their music into one genre: it is limiting. Forget preconceived notions and go for it. I have found that many of my favorite books could not be categorized into one genre. So if you wrote the scifi horror war book and are stressing over fitting it into a single genre, don't fret. You are an innovator.

Judging a Book by Its Author

When you're a newer writer, or at least new in the book publishing world, it takes more to get readers to notice you. Because put yourself in their shoes: how else are they supposed to notice you? That's why you need a stellar book cover, synopsis, and 'About the Author.'

Judging a book by its cover is normally frowned upon, but everyone does it. You have to make sure your cover reflects who you are and what your writing is. Grab your readers' attention. There are many approaches to this that can be used. Peruse Amazon's bestselling indie book section[31]. These are relatively unknown authors, who rely on their covers to gain readers before any other tactics. So see what works for them and implement it in your own cover.

Next, once your reader is attracted by your cover, they will want to know what the book is about. You cannot normally just give a brief summary without boring them until they click on the next book. You must grab them with an attention seeking call to action. Take the opening lines for the synopsis for my

---

[31] http://www.amazon.com/Best-Sellers-Kindle-Store-Indie-Books/zgbs/digital-text/3059252011

book *Notes Never Sent* for example: "Extraordinary circumstances stamp the course of an otherwise ordinary life: a child braves cancer. A nun fights against discrimination. A drug addict volunteers for the community. An immigrant learns to speak English through reading the newspaper." These phrases grab a reader. They are concise, use powerful language, and leave a reader wanting to read more.

Finally, you need to make your readers fall for you. Why will they be interested in what you have to say? For that you will want to follow this method for writing your "About the Author" section. You will want to start by simply introducing yourself with your name and where you're from. Then you can get creative. Maybe talk about when you started writing or what influences you. What sets you apart from others or on the other hand, what will make your readers relate to you?

The author's page on the back of my book looks something like this, simple and straightforward: "A literary prodigy, New Jersian Morissa Schwartz, had her first national article published in Discovery Girls Magazine at age twelve, her first job as an adviser to Junior Scholastic Magazine at thirteen, and her first book published at age seventeen. Morissa is currently a contributor for Entertainment

Weekly's Community where she has written about everything from "South Park" and "A Clockwork Orange" to her own experience in Hollywood singing on MTV. Morissa has been highlighted on Fox, Teen Kids News, MTV, Copycat, News 12, Spotlight, Let's Chat, and Infamous. She has been featured in The Huff Post, Yahoo Finance, and US News and World Report. She has written for Cambio, Medium, Hello Giggles, Writer's Cafe, Chelsea Krost, College Times, Next Step, Inside Jersey, Discovery Girls, Mad, and Scholastic."

That example is good for a more serious toned book like the one that this was for, it tells the reader who I am and why they should listen to me, but if you want to do something a little more fun and creative, you can go crazy with it, like I did with this longer author's page, that pokes fun at the tired 'About the Author' model. While something like this may be too long for the back of the book, it is perfect for an author's website:

"Morissa Schwartz was born in October, a time when pencil sales are at their lowest. People tend to buy pencils only the month before during the beginning of the school year and then when it is standardized test time, but never in October. Yet for Morissa, October was the month she would always get a new set of mechanical pencils. Every year for her birthday, she was given a new box, each one different. She received neon colored ones, mechanical pencils designed to look like number twos, red ones, ones with funny logos on them…

She would use these pencils to doodle the faces of her close friends. Then, she would draw her dogs. Her Shi-tzu would always be eating in her funny drawings. And the Maltese would always have a toy in his mouth. She would draw spirals in the margins of her notebooks and crazy shapes, which she would connect to her words and song lyrics. She would write the words to her favorite songs over and over. First, songs by the likes of Kelly Clarkson and Evanescence. Later, she'd write the words she heard Jack White and The Beatles croon. And after that, she began to produce her own words. Words that reflected her innermost thoughts and memories that she did not even know to exist.

As she got older, Morissa used these pencils to write stories. At first, she wrote a lot of fiction. Her pencil spoke of the time a talking dog named Murphy saved the town from a fire. She wrote about a talking pumpkin that didn't want to be turned into pie. She never did like pumpkin pie. Later, she used her pencil to write about three misfit middle schoolers who defy the odds and win their school's talent show.

When Morissa grew just a bit more and began to form life experiences, she would use her neon green pencil to write about those times. She wrote of her forth birthday party in a bowling alley, when her best friend at the time dropped a bowling ball on her finger and fractured it. Yet, Morissa was too busy with her own game to worry about her friend's pain and kept playing. She and that friend never spoke again after that day. Writing about the experience with her metalic pencil was Morissa's way of working through the guilt of her first friendship lost.

And when Morissa's closest relative, her great-grandmother, died, on paper she still lived. Morissa used the pink pencil her memom gave her to write about life with her special relative. Times spent singing, playing, and laughing. Happy memories.

Morissa used her sharpest pencil to write a note to her high school guidance counselor when her best friend who was being bullied said he no longer wanted to live. Her pencil may have saved a life that day.

Morissa's many pencils have come and gone. She has probably amassed thousands over the years. Her pencils are almost as fleeting as her memories would be if it weren't for the writings that they produce, which keep them alive on paper."

While this is an extreme *about the author* that is more creative non-fiction than about me, I hope it shows you that your 'about the author' doesn't have to be bland. You can get creative and have fun with it. Your readers will love you for it.

Social Media and You

Writing your book, editing it, and publishing it are not easy tasks. But there is ANOTHER step you shouldn't neglect, dear GenZer: social media promotion. It's really important.

You want your book read, and one of the most important channels is through your social media. On Facebook, let everyone know about your book. Tell them how hard you work on your writing and why they should read it. More than that, promote on LinkedIn. How many people can say they've written a book? Advertise your exceptional skills on there. A great career can come out of your book and the fact that it was published can impress the right person and company.

You should have a Twitter.[32] And despite what you may hear, it is not as 'outdated' as MySpace. In fact, it's a pretty critical tool for writers. While on Twitter, let your followers know…but be sure to follow these[33] tips so you don't come off as spam. You can even create a Facebook Fanpage or Instagram account for your book with photos of the inspiration for your book. Create a blog in the

---

[32] When you create your password, remember you need to include an uppercase character, a specialty character, a protagonist character, and a great setting. Ah, English Twitter humor.
[33] http://www.writeontrack.ie/blogs/10-tips-writers-using-twitter-effectively/

voice of your main character. Really, the options for promotion are endless. Remember to have fun with them!

Don't forget about one of your most important resources: the people you already know. Family, friends, coaches, teachers, peers...you know so many people! Let them know what you wrote. Talk face-to-face and on social media. You can send personal emails and messages to those you know. Heck, even go super old school and call Grandma. Tell her you wrote a book. She'll be so proud she'll go out and buy twenty!

There are readers who will eagerly want to read your book, but they won't always find you. That is why you need to seek them out through your own self-

Morissa Schwartz

promotion, because in the end, you know your writing and own personal audience's taste better than anyone. You worked so hard on your writing, so why not let your friends, family, fans, and prospective employers see?

Write Expert

You and your writing are more important than you may even realize. Peter Handke once said, "If a nation loses its storytellers, it loses its childhood." That is why you, writers, are so important. You are who will make a difference. You are who the world depends on to make sense of it. That is why writers are so special.

Well, there you have it. You read the book. You have your tools. You're ready to have a hit book. Just don't forget about me when you're a bestselling author!

I'd love to connect with you on Twitter @Feefeertr and @GenZPub. And visit GenZPublishing.org for tips and publishing opportunities. You can also check in and say 'hi' on my website MorissaSchwartz.com. Happy writing!

Morissa Schwartz

Bonus

Don't just take my advice into account. Great authors also have some pretty interesting things to say about the writing process. Here are some great quotes and advice from those we most love to read:

"Who wants to become a writer? And why? Because it's the answer to everything. ... It's the streaming reason for living. To note, to pin down, to build up, to create, to be astonished at nothing, to cherish the oddities, to let nothing go down the drain, to make something, to make a great flower out of life, even if it's a cactus."

—Enid Bagnold

"Write. Rewrite. When not writing or rewriting, read. I know of no shortcuts."

—Larry L. King, WD

"People say, 'What advice do you have for people who want to be writers?' I say, they don't really need advice, they know they want to be writers, and they're gonna do it. Those people who know that they really want to do this and are cut out for it, they know it."

—R.L. Stine, WD

'Writing for the New Generation' is a GenZ™ Publishing.

GenZ™ is an innovative publishing platform for the new generation to have their work seen, recognized, published and read by millions. When an individual is chosen to be published on GenZ™, they can use that experience in their portfolios, for résumés, to share with friends, family, and fans. It is an accomplishment to be proud of for the rest of their lives.

We are on a mission to improve the world one word at a time. That is why we are the place for voices to be heard in a way not previously done in print and on digital media. It is a way to support young writers, our new voices.

It can be nearly impossible for young writers with promising talent to produce standout work that will be recognized, because of the state of the publishing and digital media industries. Having work recognized in a sea of so many writers is even tougher. That is why there is an underrepresentation of young and innovative voices in the publishing and print world. There are many unheard voices. GenZ is on a mission to change that.

GenZ™ provides a medium where these people can be positively recognized for their work through a professional product and supportive company.

Learn more about GenZ Publishing, how you can get involved, and all of our newest releases at GenZPublishing.org. Like us on Facebook at GenZ Publishing and follow us on Twitter @GenZPub.

Morissa Schwartz

www.ingramcontent.com/pod-product-compliance
Lightning Source LLC
Chambersburg PA
CBHW080447110426
42743CB00016B/3311